MW01273502

Networked Youth

What <u>Every</u> Parent *Needs* to Know About Online Behaviour

JOHN D. TYLER

Foreward by Jesse Miller, Social Media Expert and Strategist

Joe,
I always appreciate your advice
and friendship! John

Networked Youth: What Every Parent Needs to Know About Online Behaviour

First Printing, June 2016

ISBN: 978-0-9951785-0-2

DEDICATION

To the Little General – I appreciate that you always call it like it is – whether I want to hear it or not.

FORWARD BY JESSE MILLER

The Internet, now more than ever before, is capable of supporting the vast and diverse range of individual communications within online social networking. The Internet has established itself as the foundation of social and business communications where users participate by transferring gigabytes of information on a second-by-second basis to convey personal events through digital medias. A by-product of this constant information sharing is the school and home-based conversations of Internet safety and social media awareness specifically designed to educate the youth who use these services and technologies on a daily basis to connect with friends and popular culture events.

This topic of online safety has engaged media circles, been embraced by parent groups, become the focus of numerous public safety announcements, and while much attention is given to the online activities of young people on social media sites like Facebook, a large majority of the current theories of social media use fail to account for the unique vantage point that educators have in this developing topic. Their perspective is incredibly important as the realities of social media use and networked communications reflect the daily lives of individuals and adds the perspective and context that educators see as mobile technologies enter schools, classrooms, and the offices of school administrators.

As the content generated by youth and shared online influences the conversations of peers within schools and extra-curricular activities, the vantage point of where social media and online communications have influenced daily on goings within schools is incredibly important for parents to understand as the generational shift has taken the activities and angst of adolescence and made it openly available to the world via the Internet.

Social media communications have fundamentally altered the practices of information-sharing and online visibility for youth and have now given kids a world stage through multiple mediums to post and share the ongoing of their developing lives. What becomes a concern for parents and educators is how these communications impact the traditional participation expectations and development of youth in their learning environments. As social media offers affordances to communication that previous generations would have been entirely envious of as teens - whether it be the want for privacy in communications or in the actions of by-passing parental supervision of telecommunications or media consumption - the uses of social sharing, online gaming, video and audio download, and access to information online is entirely a wonderful technological development. Ironically, as wonderful as the progress of connectivity is, if you ask the majority of parents and adults ranging from Boomers to Generation-X if they are happy that they had a childhood before the Internet existed in its current ubiquitous form, they will happily tell you that the past deserves to be buried in the past far away from digital record.

Bearing in mind the numerous affordances of social media technologies, the wondrous abilities do not further preclude individual control over story telling and information sharing. Youth can have their content "go viral" over the course of an evening before they return home at curfew, a hyper-sexualized text can be sent as innocently and as quickly as a trip to the washroom, and chronic text communication can interrupt sleep, study, and a family dinner.

Despite these concerns, it is important for parents to overcome the shock, the frustrations, and distinct contrast in generational divide and recognize that social media technologies primarily follow trending themes that presume individual information control where many young users believe that as long as they control the mobile device, they control the online content. Parents require more than an understanding of popular communications, they have to be prepared to accept that their want for control of how their children access content or in their want for censorship is far beyond what parents of previous generations had as it applied to old media content such as television, video, or telecommunications.

With online connectivity in mind, youth (who traditionally represent a vulnerable sector within our populations), shape the communication dynamics of social media applications sites and force peers to alter their approach to online based communications to account for the networked and on-demand nature of social media. As social media is often behind public concern over inappropriate or harmful content being directed towards impressionable youth, it behooves parents to learn more about how and when youth are engaging online and to learn from the social media hiccups that have impacted young adults since the introduction of social media communications.

There are a number of books available that address these issues but in choosing to read this book in particular, it is important to reflect as you read that this writing starts where the author who as an educator, a school administrator, and most importantly a parent has put the effort to provide a positive foundational understanding from his own perspectives and experiences to help parents fully understand how, when, and where youth are communicating online and how they are building a culture of Internet sharing using social media platforms to continue dialogues outside traditional communication boundaries.

As an educator, John has provided the unique experiences he has seen in how technologies have influenced the classroom, how student focus, alertness, and class participation has changed the dynamics of education. This book clearly highlights where the benefits exist as schools explore the uses of bring your own device policies and in contrast where the problems stem from access of chronic communications and how parental abdication of oversight can cause a single youth life event to become an overnight online viral sensation.

What is of unique benefit within the chapters of this book is that you are seeing the perspective of the educator and school administrator who has throughout his career had the betterment of the child at heart. As I read through this book,

I felt at times that I was in the Principal's office, helping the child understand cause and effect of social sharing, reflecting on the consequences and resources available when an online sharing moment has turned into a community conversation, and where youth can not only explore the Internet with friends and online peers but to fully understand how the human nature of social media sharing trumps the perspectives of online privacy.

It is important to establish how online identity is shaped as youth engage via social media and within the chapters of this book, you will learn more about the connected world your children or the children you work with are coping. The connected culture of chronic connectivity and sharing of life events may seem daunting or ridiculous to some but it is the world our children are born into and although I am entirely envious of a world where questions can be answered via search engine, I am entirely happy I had a childhood well before social media existed – that being said, raising children in the connected world requires engaged parenting, reflective thoughts, seeing and accepting a different point of view, and respecting the words of wonderful teachers who experience the impacts of the social media teen on a daily basis with every app and new communication trend.

CONTENTS

INTRODUCTION

If you have picked up this book then you have taken a big step in acknowledging that you want to help guide kids in making good decisions when using the Internet and interacting online. As adults, we did not grow up using the social media tools that kids use today - let alone having unlimited and often unfiltered access to millions of websites and people with the click of a button or swipe of a finger. The good news is that you are not alone. Parents and teachers alike are searching for ways to start, and continue conversations with kids about the appropriate use of digital devices.

Our parents taught us the values, norms, and manners important in their time to become good citizens. Today, I see parents, teachers and adults trying to share those same lessons with kids. But a new type of citizenship has emerged – *Digital Citizenship*. Think about that term and what it means to you. In general, the behaviours we expect from kids when they are online are similar to the values our parents tried to instill in us. We want kids to treat others well, be authentic and share positive information (all the good stuff) when they share things online. For the most part, from what I see everyday in schools; our kids do a tremendous job of treating each other with respect and kindness when they are face to face. Unfortunately, much of the time their interactions are not face-to-face, but done so in *the cloud*.

The cloud is such an appropriate term because the people we interact with can be very close to us in proximity or relationship, yet they also seem nowhere near us. They can seem as far away as when we look up at the clouds. This distance often makes us feel like we can say things anonymously or at least without the repercussions that we might deal with if we said those same things directly to someone's face. It all seems like common sense so far – so why do you need this book?

As we jump into this world, take a minute to gauge your thoughts on the following questions:

1. What does it mean to take responsibility and to be respectful in your offline and online world in order to be a good digital citizen?
2. What are the consequences if you are irresponsible or disrespectful in the face-to-face world? What about in the online world?
3. What is one important responsibility you have in your online world?
4. What is a responsibility you have in common in both your offline and online world?
5. What are your coping tools if you are the victim of any disrespectful behaviour?

As adults, the majority of us don't have enough experience using devices and interacting online to root our advice in our own mistakes. In many cases, I've seen adults posting things online and making the same mistakes that kids make; the kind that we would describe as inappropriate when trying to explain to kids what is acceptable and what is offside regarding online behaviour. I've made these same mistakes also over the years, as has my wife, friends and other family members. The reality is that we are trying to guide kids today in scenarios and communicate in ways that are new to us. We are not only learning at the same time as kids, but in many cases, they are exposed and familiar to many more types of social media tools than we are. The resulting gap has sometimes led to labeling both children and parents. Kids are often described as *Digital Natives* while Adults are the *Digital Immigrants/Explorers.*

So how can we guide them? There is a great deal of debate amongst my colleagues on the answer to this question. Educator Brad Ovenell-Carter, suggested to me that we should be on any social media site our kids are using regularly. At the very least, we should know about how to use the site. He questions whether our childrens' use of Social Media platforms is any different than if they were taking a trip or going on a sleep-over. If your child says they are staying at a friend's house and you have never met this friend, what is your response? Do you want to meet the friend? Meet the friends' parents? Know if the parents will be home? By familiarizing ourselves with the world in which our kids are interacting on a daily , if not hourly, basis we can be better equipped to help them when challenges do arise.

While there are concerns to be aware of when connecting with others online; I am, by no means, condemning online interaction. As you work through this book and the embedded activities, there are three key considerations we need to consider about our childrens' behaviour whether it be online or offline.:

1. How do they want to be perceived?

2. Who do they want to be?

3. How do they want to influence the world?

Social networking sites have many positive benefits, one of which is defining how a generation is building networks that will impact them for many years to come. These networks supplement friendships as long as users understand and mitigate these three risks: 1) building and maintaining a positive online reputation; 2) keeping information private; and 3) balancing online activities with real-life pursuits. Personally, I love and see great value in social media and online interaction!

1

WHAT GOES AROUND COMES AROUND

Suddenly, you hear your teen and his friends talking about something from an APP, the likes of which you have never heard. Your daughter and a friend are arguing about something one of them posted online, but you have no idea where. Alternatively, kids in your classes make plans without ever talking on the phone and best you can tell, they are going to a party at the house of someone who goes by the name of @citygirl. What happened? As parents, we question why they used to share everything with you, and now they are sharing things with everyone but you, and the worst part is; you realize you don't even know what or where they are posting this stuff. How are they doing these things?

You may be sitting there thinking *I can't believe that I've become my parents.* I understand. I have a teenage daughter and I work with teenagers all day, everyday. We aren't like our parents were. We are hip, we let your kids' friends call us by our first names and in fact; as teachers, even some kids call us by first names. Even if they don't use the first name, we are still cool enough because we use the internet and we have smart phones. We even stream movies and read books on an eReader!

If any of the above sounds familiar, don't worry; you aren't alone. The reality is that every generation of adults has felt that they have lost touch with what is cool. Maybe you used to hang out and have sleep overs with friends while renting a series of bad horror videos – yes, I said videos because likely there were no DVD's when you were a teen – and I speak from experience! Maybe you used to get together at the local football game on a Friday night. Now when you go there, teenagers' faces are buried in their phones. Whatever you did for fun as a teen, you are probably feeling like it is NOT what kids are doing today.

Now, kids do everything online. For example, they don't rent movies, they stream them online. If they do rent them, they don't go to the local video store and hope that the new release is available. Rather, they watch it on Pay-Per-View instantly, whenever they feel like it. I know this, because I've seen the bills and likely you have too – or at least you know someone who has had this experience. If you are teacher - in the past you might have tried to rent a specific movie, while now kids offer to download it or explain that you can stream it online.

At some point as adults, whatever the moment has been; you've likely asked yourself when and how did everything become so instantaneous. If you are like me, then you love the benefits and conveniences of technology. At the same time, I've wondered what negative impact this way of life may have on kids growing up in this world. They don't learn to sit and wait patiently for their favorite song to come on the radio so that they can tape it. They don't have to save up all of their money to buy the record, tape or CD only to get home and find they only like 1 or 2 songs. Instead, they listen ahead of time and buy the 1 or 2 songs they like. Everything that kids are learning about technology has a lot to do with instant gratification. Along with developing a thirst for instant sense of gratification comes the instant decision-making, unfortunately sometimes at the expense of judgement.

The Other Group

Some are likely reading this thinking that none of that stuff applies to them. They think, I know what kids do online. I know what sites my kids use and I talk to them about their life online. They don't keep secrets from me. Why is he telling me about parenting stuff when this book is supposed to be about keeping kids safe online? I want him to teach me how to help kids make good choices online.

I used to think this way as well. Working in a high school everyday, I like to think that I am pretty tuned in to what kids are doing online. I hear about the sites on which they share information. I know what Apps they are using. Sometimes it surprises my teen, just how much I know about what is going on. Despite all of this, I was pretty surprised to find her activity on a certain site. She seemed to be handling herself well, but it was tough to see people posting negative things online about my child. I would be lying saying it doesn't sting when someone calls her "fake" and "a bitch". Seeing her post profile pics where I wish she wore less make-up or where I could see she was trying to look "older" was equally tough. All of these things were happening regardless of the regular conversations I'd had with her about posting online.

I had to take a step back and put this into context. My wife helped when she told me about times she would wait until she got to school to put on make-up or certain outfits. These examples reminded me that kids' behavior today is really no different than previous generations. Today, it is *how* they communicate that has changed. We used to pass notes in class, now they text. We used to take pictures and wait patiently for them to be developed, now kids take "selfies" – repeating and deleting until they are happy; then editing, cropping and filtering before sharing with *x number* of friends - in a moment. The human nature has not changed; what has is the speed at which our kids are making decisions.

The Good News

It doesn't matter which of these two groups to which you belong. None of what is outlined here is tied to whether you feel you are a good parent or teacher. Nor is it connected to being hip and cool as an adult. It's not even directly connected to being open and communicative. The fact that you are reading this does NOT suggest that you don't know what to do. It simply means that your kids are like the 100's of millions of other kids around the world who communicate and connect with their friends using some web or technology based method. The reality is that none of this existed when we grew up and so we could benefit from having additional tools in our tool-belts to help our kids navigate in this world. That's okay.

Protecting our children from harm online is just as important as it is in the real world. While modeling good behaviour as a parent is important, is equally important that we play a vital role in helping children have safe and positive experiences online. Utilizing Internet allows experiences we never had growing up. These can be social, educational, or purely for entertainment. No matter for what purpose our kids go online, there are risks and challenges. They can encounter inappropriate material, sexually explicit content or even exposure to that which is violent and illegal. Whatever it is that they find, whether they seek it out or stumble across it by accident; we need to take an active role in talking with kids about how to respond to this entire world of choices that they will encounter at an increasingly young age.

The reason for this book and why I took time to relay this information is that a disconnect exists. Certainly that's a blanket statement that's not taking into account the great examples that I see, but make no mistake; Everyday, there are good kids making poor decisions online. These are the same great kids that are fantastic at handling face to face situations. These are some of the same kids whom are respectful, courteous, and kind all around. But they are also kids for whom there is a disconnect at times, between these same great behaviours and their online life. And as we know with the internet, it only takes one post; one quick moment in time for your child to become an online sensation. By talking to our kids about these risks and rewards and by answering their questions and concerns, we can help to try and keep them safe and make good choices when they are online. Let's start by looking at our own online behaviours.

2

THE REARVIEW MIRROR

Okay, so we've established that most of us are on the same page in terms of our own past experiences and current challenges guiding children today. Just like you thought your parents had no idea about anything remotely cool, it is an inevitable cycle that your kids would think the same. The important part is that you are not helpless. The next few chapters are designed to help you put a plan in place to help your kids make better decisions.

Many people think that this is an easy fix. Their solution is to simply ban children from being on certain sites. Some people will buy their kids a phone but refuse to add a data package thinking this will prevent them from going to sites where the negative behavior happens. The problem with this line of thinking is the same as through previous generations. Think about when you have told your kids you don't like certain friends - do they always listen and stop hanging out with those kids? Probably not – they likely just hide these friendships at least until they decide on their own terms that those friends are not the people with whom they wish to associate.

Shakespeare's *Romeo and Juliet* was written hundreds of years ago, but the theme has stood the test of time for many reasons and is still current today. Maybe your parents told you not to date that guy who had the motorcycle. Maybe they told you they didn't like you dating that girl who smoked – I know mine did. Whatever the reason, with many teens; the moment you tell them one thing, they will dig in and do another. This is part of the behavior of growing up and making your own mistakes in order to learn your own lessons.

Kids today are no different with this behavior than they were 10, 20, 50 years ago, I'll guess. If you tell them not to go online, not to use a certain site, not to do anything, there is a chance they will listen, but there is a far greater chance that they will say 'okay Dad', then leave the house and do the exact opposite. Besides that, do you think a little thing like no data package on their phone will stop them? They will access Internet at a friend's, at school, even at a grocery store or coffee shop. There is free Wifi in pretty much any store, let alone school, or at their friends' houses.

The heart of the issue is not when and where they can access Internet. The heart of the issue lies in being equipped to make good choices when they are online. We've often said that mistakes are for learning. We expect kids to make mistakes. Unfortunately, mistakes made in the online world have a tendency to have longer standing and broader consequences. This is very difficult for us as adults. The heart of our concern is that these mistakes are now often exposed to hundreds, thousands or even millions of people because of the way we share information. So rather than banning devices, sites or Internet usage altogether; we need to have conversations about how they are using Internet. What they are posting on their profiles and with whom they are sharing so much of their lives.

Again, some people may think this is easy. 'All I have to do is make deal with my child that they will add me to their sites'. 'If we are friends then we can each share openly'. This can work when kids are younger. As kids get older, this just is not practical, let alone realistic. When you were a teenager, did you want your parents listening in on your phone conversations? What about when you had a sleepover and wanted to talk about someone you had a crush on? Nope, you probably didn't want mom and dad in on that conversation either. Well, your kids are no different – they don't want you involved in every detail of their lives either. This is not to say that we should never connect with our children online. This can be a great start to help them learn about Social Media. However, as a long-term solution this plan may be viewed as nothing more than policing kids, which is exactly what they don't want. Has your child ever said "Don't you trust me"? Odds are you do trust your kids but we've established the magnitude of potential mistakes.

Beth and Dan

My friend and colleague, Jesse Miller, shared with me the story of Beth and Dan. Beth was a strong student, who made great decisions, got good grades and dated Dan, the quarterback of the football team. Nothing bad in this story happens: Beth doesn't run away with Dan or get pregnant and Dan doesn't drive under the influence of drugs or alcohol, ending in hurting or killing anyone. The problem in Beth and Dan's story is that no one talked to either of them about things like sexting and sharing pictures. After dating for nearly a year, Dan asked Beth to send a topless picture. Beth reluctantly agreed. Just before she sent the message, she texted, "I'm really nervous – do you promise you won't send it to anyone else?" Dan meant what he said when he responded that, "I promise I won't". With the click of a few buttons, Beth sent the picture. In just seconds, she heard a yell from upstairs. "Beth get in here right now". You see Beth had sent the picture to *Dad* and not *Dan*.

The learning here was far safer than if her boyfriend had been immature and sent the pics to friends. It could have been even worse if she and Dan had broken up and he posted them online for the world to see – something that has happened to countless people. I think in the moment, Beth would probably have preferred either scenario as opposed to her **DAD** seeing her topless! Fortunately for Beth, this little error taught her a lifetime's worth of lessons without a lifetime of online humiliation. Beth even went on to share this story to her entire grad class during a lesson on the importance of protecting their online reputations.

The story of Beth and Dan is real. People do things regularly on Internet that begs one question, "What were you thinking?". Most importantly, it does not just happen to kids.

Justine

If you haven't heard of Justine Sacco and her story, it is one with which you should be aware. Justine had a relatively small social network - some online reports suggest it was around 200 followers on Twitter when she made a huge mistake and sent a very inappropriate tweet. Despite her small following things moved around the world very quickly. In the few hours it took for her flight to travel from the US to her homeland of South Africa, her life would be changed - forever.

When her flight left, Justine was a successful PR executive who was flying home to see her family in South Africa for the holidays. Before boarding her 12 hour flight, Justine tweeted 'Going to Africa. Hope I don't get AIDS. Just Kidding. I'm White!' What Justine had no idea about was the fact that the post was re-tweeted over **3,000** times and it was picked up by media outlets around the world. For the entire twelve hours in the air, Sacco remained completely unaware that her life was unraveling. There is an old saying, "what goes up, must come down" and that is exactly what happened to Justine Sacco. When she landed, the situation had gone viral on Internet. People were waiting to take her photo. And shortly after landing she was fired from her job. Online reports indicated that she spent the next several months "in hiding".

The stories of Beth, Dan and Justine could be brushed off. You could say they deserved what they got for making such bad choices. And to a certain point, you are right. And from another point of view, the reality is these mistakes are a result of human nature. Don't believe me? Take stock. When you were younger, how many mistakes did you make when you liked someone? Consider the rumours in high school about the girl that got to third base (or further). Ring a bell? How about the number of times that someone made an inappropriate comment or shared a joke about certain religions or race. I'm not condoning any of this behaviour, nor am I trying to excuse the actions in either story. These stories are two of not hundreds, but thousands of similar mistakes made by previous generations, whereas now, the people involved were not just victims of their own indiscretions, but of the speed with which their stories travelled.

That's not going to be my kid!

As I see it; if you don't want your kids to become the examples of stories like the ones in this book, then you need to make a few choices. I see good kids make bad decisions every day - literally, every day. I say that a lot to both kids and parents.

1. Choose not to ignore the fact that your child is capable of making equally bad (if not worse) choices.

2. Choose to talk about their behaviour on an ongoing basis and give them examples of how social media can destroy lives AND/OR create hugely successful lives depending on how they use it.

3. Choose to look routinely for teachable moments that illustrate: while something negative can spread very quickly; likewise, something positive can do the same.

4. Choose to have a conversation about how your child wants to be seen and perceived when it comes to Digital Citizenship.

Hopefully, these first steps will help you and your family move the conversation forward toward helping kids be good *Digital* Citizens, and further, toward becoming great *Digital Leaders*. Our kids can do not only meaningfully good things using social media, but make a positive impact on others as well.

Depending on your level of comfort with social media you may be feeling nervous, or perhaps you had no idea about how far and fast posts can travel. No matter where you land on the spectrum, I can assure you that:

(a) You should be a little on edge as these stories happen every day.

(b) These stories happen to *good* kids.

(c) You probably really aren't that far behind or out of touch with the online places your kids spend their hours; and no, it's not too late to provide guidance and tools to help your kids be safe in navigating whichever APPs and Sites they are connecting with others.

I work in schools with teenagers every day. The following chapters have a series of stories that have happened in schools, and similar stories continue to happen on a regular basis. I am sharing these with you and I encourage you to work through the activities at the end of each chapter as these are designed to help you initiate conversations with your kids about their online behaviour.

3

CONNECTED WORLD

We've established that we are in a world where people are connected 24 hours a day, 7 days a week. Not just with the friends we spend time with, but to others whom we have never met. We expect to be connected to our friends, our work and our loved ones. For many of us as parents, teachers and adults - we fear that our kids are lacking the social graces that our generation and those before us thought were important. What we need to realize is that we are imposing our beliefs of what is right to a generation that communicates and connects in a completely different manner than that which we've been accustomed.

Our kids message, trade pics and video call people from mobile devices whenever and wherever they might be. We didn't grow up this way and this is where we have room to be more open to how technology is changing communication. While we can't impose our belief system onto our kids' digital behavior - try as we may - we CAN learn and discuss with them, the implications of what they choose to do and how they choose to act in this digital world. There is good news. Even though our generation was not taught how to handle this instant communication, there are many avenues to learn how to stay up to speed. The next few chapters will provide activities for you to figure out how much you know and steps you can take to keep up with your kids.

I have heard of the Internet being compared to a loaded gun. The analogy has gone further with the now infamous NRA's slogan "guns don't kill people, people kill people." For social media, the parallel saying is, "Internet doesn't embarrass people, people on Internet embarrass people". We need to take a more global approach to teaching kids how to use Internet safely. Let's compare teaching/learning about social media to teaching young people how to drive. To get a driver's license, kids study a book, write a test and then learn to drive slowly with little practice. At least we know how to drive before teaching our kids. For the most part, we have done a lot less with our children and how they connect with others. The majority of parents think that all it takes for safe Internet use is common sense. If that were enough to stop us from bad decisions, I'd have made a lifetime of better choices!

If we take the same approach let's break this down further with a look at Australian educator Dan Haesler's thoughts:

1. Driving lessons would be taught by adults with very little or no experience.

2. Driving lessons would focus only on what not to do.

3. Driving lessons would NEVER take place in an actual car.[1]

When you see such an approach in black and white, it becomes pretty clear that we are really giving our kids that loaded gun while we stand by letting it happen.

What is holding us back?

I've laid out our challenges as parents and teachers. As adults, for the most part we are doing kids a disservice. Although it is unintentional, we can do better. Let's get over our fear if we're not up to speed in understanding how the technology our kids are using, works. We are putting our heads in the sand if we simply try to pretend that its okay not to be more knowledgeable. This doesn't mean we need to be afraid of what is out there in the world of Internet - we need to go find out for ourselves.

Most adults in the 25 - 60 years of age category have an online profile somewhere. Whether it's a photo sharing site to see pictures posted by our friends and relatives, a video conferencing site where we talk to family, or a social media site where we dabble in what the kids are using today - many of us are connected and feeling proud that we know how to use this *stuff.*

Unfortunately, just using technology is not enough. I think of a teacher with whom I worked. She was a mom of a 5 year old and she spent her entire day with teens that immersed themselves in using various forms of social media. One day we had a group of her kids writing an online exam. Following the exam, we spoke with the kids. We found out what they liked and didn't like about the electronic program. During the conversation, one of the kids said he liked the feature that allowed him to highlight what he had written. The teacher asked how he knew that is what it did. The boy responded that he just clicked the button to see what it would do. The teacher was impressed and told him that she would have been too scared, fearing that she might erase everything she had written; therefore, she wouldn't have touched any buttons unless she was told what they did.

This is not a knock on that teacher. This is a reality of how many adults approach technology. I've heard more than my mother say, "I clicked a button and everything disappeared". Today's kids are commonly referred to as *digital natives*. To limit this term to a generation of kids is ridiculous. I can tell you that there is nothing about technology that gives kids a leg up in how to use it, than what we have as adults – other than the fact that they're using it constantly. We adults can be *digital natives as well, however;* we are often held back by our fear of the unknown.

In order to eliminate some of that unknown, let's look at the first activity. To do this you will need to open a search engine on Internet – although it doesn't matter which one you use there is a belief that *Google* will likely provide you with the most responses.

ACTIVITY #1

1. Make a list of all the places you think you might appear online. Think of things like your Facebook profile, your flickr or Instagram accounts.

2. Now search your own name and make a list of all the sites where you find yourself. If you have a more common name you may need to narrow your search by adding details about yourself. For example, you may need to add the name of the city in which you live. I share the name of a former president of the United States. I could bury my head in the sand and say to myself, "looks good, there is nothing on the first couple of pages". The reality is, if I look deep enough or specifically enough, there they are – pages and pages of my life, open and available for anyone to see.

Were you surprised at the snapshot of your own life that was available?

3. Try the same search process but find your child's or children's name(s). Now make a list of the sites that they appear on.

Did these results surprise you? Don't just take note of the sites on which they appear, but take the time to observe what type of activity in which they engage.

4. Think long and hard about the search results. If any of your own behavior surprised you, then don't be too critical of what your children are doing. You have to clean up your own act before you can deal with your kids.

5. While the following step could be the toughest, it is the most important. Repeat step 2 but do it together WITH your child or children. They may tell you it's creepy; they may tell you no; they may even tell you that you don't have the right to do that. In all cases they are wrong. Let them know that this is no different than what a prospective employer will do. It is also no different than any scholarship or awards committee does. For that matter, it is even no different than what a prospective date will likely do!

What you have just done is uncover your *Digital Footprints*. The simplest way to think of this is that every time you log in to something online, you leave an imprint. Unlike your foot in the sand, this imprint does not wash away. There is always a trace of where you have been.

If you uncover anything you don't like, there are often steps that can be taken to limit the negatives that you have unearthed. You don't need to delete entire accounts (although sometimes that is not out of the question). You or your child can delete posts, pictures and videos – however, not always if these appear on other people's accounts.

Some tips that are commonly used by educators in order to help kids be proactive from this point on include:

- Never post anything that you might find embarrassing later. This can be tough for kids because many haven't developed a sufficient enough filter to fully realize future implications – this is where your guidance can be important.
- Be careful with the pictures you post on your public profiles. Remember that others will see them and judge

you based on their content.

- Change the privacy settings on your social networking sites so that only your Friends can see your information.
- Do not disclose your personal address, phone number, passwords, bank card/credit card numbers and so on, even in private messages. There is always the possibility of somebody hacking into your account and finding them. Just read about a few celebrities recently, having had inappropriate photos stolen!
- Do not post things to bully, hurt, blackmail, insult, or afflict any kind of harm on others.

That last one may seem like common sense but remember, we are talking about youth and especially when we deal with teenagers, who haven't fully reached their capacity for or development of common sense. The immediate nature of posting online is too consuming for them to stop and think about the impact of their actions. The important thing to remember is that once information has been posted online, it is virtually impossible to remove because of archiving and file sharing. Even though you de-activate or completely delete your accounts, the information may still be retrieved by others and in many cases is owned by the site you are using. Take the time to read terms of agreement and not just when you sign up but regularly, over a period of time, as they may change.

The most important lesson to learn is that although you may not be able to delete things that have been posted, you can change behavior so that future, inappropriate stuff doesn't end up out there in the digital world. But no matter what the age of your child, I encourage you NOT to eliminate their access to Internet all together.

4

HOW *UNLIMITED* IS THIS CONNECTED WORLD?

It has been mentioned several times about the limits of saying NO to your children when it comes to their access to Internet and their digital connections. There have been restrictions on children and teen behaviours for decades, if not centuries. Just as technology has evolved at a rapid rate over the past several years, so has the way in which kids expect to be treated. They have access to worldwide information with connections at their fingertips and with that access we need to treat them with greater rights and responsibilities than previous generations. Most educators and other adults who spend significant hours with kids will tell you that the majority will rise to meet your expectations. Now that they have unlimited potential, it is even more important than ever that we set the bar high when it comes to our expectations of their connected behavior.

The last chapter and exercise had us explore the Digital Footprint. Here we will explore relationships and communication.

In 2011, a Nielson report indicated that the average teen sends over 3,000 texts a month. [2]

That's right, I will type that again 3,000 texts/month. This does not include messages they send through Facebook or tweets on Twitter, never mind any of the SnapChat messages they send! It is very clear that kids have changed the way they communicate.

What happened to talking on the phone for hours?

Some of you may be thinking back to the times when you would talk to a friend for hours at a time. Yes, some of that conversation was ridiculous - I know I did it too, but it was one of the ways we communicated. I guarantee that there were parents or grandparents questioning what we did on the phone for all that time. They were asking themselves, "why can't they talk in person like we used to?"

In many ways, as a parent it is probably easier if your child talks on the phone. At least if they are talking, we can glean some idea of the conversation from the bits that we overhear. With messaging, we have no idea who they are texting, let alone the nature of the messages. If we ask, kids will often tell us that we wouldn't understand. Sound familiar?

When we judge kids today for how they communicate, we are placing our expectations and past societal norms on their behavior. That is not fair to them. They communicate differently with their friends than we did. There is a far bigger issue than the fact that the way they communicate bugs us. They are learning on their own how to navigate relationships online.

We established earlier in the book that many of us do not have the social media experience to pass along to our kids. I have seen more fights and arguments in my time in schools as a result of something that was posted online. Many times the posts are directed at a single person. They are threats or contain nasty innuendos. Often, these are the types of rumours that were spread when we went to school, but now people will post things directly about others. Your child might not receive the message directly but things could be said about them on others' pages. These hurtful comments are often expressions that would never be said face to face, but are easily typed and sent out to the world without a second thought.

Lisa and Adrienne

There is the story of Lisa and Adrienne. Growing up they were good friends. Upon entering High School, Adrienne met new friends and for a while Lisa was part of the new group. As Adrienne became closer with her new friends she, like many teenagers, didn't know how to tell Lisa that they had grown apart. So instead of having a conversation, the new group of girls began posting inappropriate things onto Lisa's social media accounts. Lisa didn't respond...at first. After a while, as Lisa felt more and more alone she became increasingly hurt and angry. When she finally responded, she did it with one tweet - less than 140 characters during first period Science class. By the end of class most of the kids in school knew about it and the boys were salivating for a fight. In the halls on the way to class, Lisa and Adrienne passed each other. They hadn't spoken directly to each other in weeks. Despite that, with the encouragement of the other kids, they were quickly encircled with little space to move. Before either of them knew it, they were rolling on the floor scratching each other and pulling the other's hair. All of this happened as they were surrounded by hundreds of their classmates, several of them using their phones to video the incident to live on forever through various social media sites. Their relationship was now over, all because they couldn't communicate in person.

Stories similar to that of Lisa and Adrienne have been played out in every school and through every year I have worked for the past several years. I guarantee it is played out at countless schools around the world and the basics of the story are all the same. Someone says something, there is a response and it escalates like a game. Our School Liason police officers deal with threats made through social media on a regular basis and despite educating one group or grade; a new grade comes in and they are as poorly prepared to navigate these relationships as the last.

But what can I do?

There is good news.

"Research shows that the majority of kids' online relationships are with people they already know and in general; contrary to adult concerns, time spent online does not mean they are spending less face-to-face time with their friends. Social media, it turns out, actually facilitates and can even strengthen offline interaction!"[3]

If you are confident that your child likely is not connecting with strangers, we can focus on some steps that you can take to help them navigate those relationships with the people they do know. Banning your child from using certain sites is not the answer. Have conversations about what sites they are on. Have occasional Social Media Health checks where you sit down with your child and review their online profiles together. Just like you would have a conversation with your child about choosing "good" friends. It is important to talk about expectations of behaviours online. Talk to them about how you expect them to treat others. Remember we said in the opening chapters that face to face interactions generally have not changed. Let them know that you expect them to behave in the same fashion online as one would, face to face. If they try to tell you that you don't understand, don't accept that. Let them know that you might not know the tools they are using but, you understand and expect the same behaviours online as in person.

ACTIVITY # 2

Whether you answer the questions in point form or write them out, it is important to take the time to actually really think about these questions and record your responses. These questions will help guide you in your discussions with kids down the road and help you form your thoughts on what it means to be a *Digital Citizen* and *Digital Leader*.

1. What does it mean to take responsibility and to be respectful in your offline and online world in order to be a good digital citizen?
2. What are the consequences if you are irresponsible or disrespectful in the face-to-face world? What about in the online world?
3. What is one important responsibility you have in your online world?
4. What is a responsibility you have in common in both your offline and online world?

We've established that everything we post online—and everything that others post about us—contributes to our permanent, digital reputation. Most of what we have focused on has surrounded the negative. There is a lot that we can be proud of online when the stories are positive and that we will cover in the next chapter. Good or bad, it is important to help our kids understand that everything online is searchable, replicable and can be viewed by unlimited audiences. Whether it's a tweet or a photo: if it has been posted - it can be searched forever. Worse, that means it can be copied and shared by anyone. Kids can't be expected to fully understand the enormity of all their choices but it is important for families to talk about managing their online reputations and to agree on guidelines for behavior.

5

REPUTATION

The old saying, 'the apple doesn't fall far from the tree' could not be more relevant than when it comes to a kid's online reputation. This could be the toughest chapter for you and it's important that parents understand the enormity of what I am going to share with you in the next few paragraphs. Your behaviour online will have a strong, if not the strongest, impact in shaping your children's behavior. If you don't believe me, then think about driving with your kids. You are late and you get frustrated – so you lash out at another driver, maybe flip them the middle finger and then a few days later your 5 year old is giving the same gesture to another kid in class. Where do you think your child learned the behavior? Certainly these impressions are more profound the younger the child, but learned behavior from home has a very profound impact at any age – good and bad. Yes, they learn things at school. They learn things on the playground. They learn things from friends with whom they hang out. Likewise, kids absorb what we do and they will also absorb what and how we post online. This extends to frequency and use and what is implied as acceptable.

It is important to help kids understand that everything online is pervasive, persistent, searchable, replicable and can be viewed by vast, invisible audiences. [4] In other words, that photo posted of you at the party with a lampshade on your head? Yes, it stays in the digital world FOREVER. It may have seemed like a lot of fun at the time, and no harm may have come from it in later years, but it can still to this day be searched for and found by anyone and everyone. It can be copied, shared, edited and viewed by strangers around the world. Ouch! Think of the impact that could have on us all as we apply for jobs. Now multiply that impact as kids walk the halls at school. We are no longer in the age where stories develop into rumours that are spread around school, whether they are accurate or inaccurate. When positive, it's great, but when not, it can be disastrous. A recent Huffington Post article summed this up perfectly - "Drunk driving literally ends lives. But digital drama can potentially end a bright future for your child and their dreams."[5]

Right or wrong, good or bad; the core behavior of teens hasn't changed. If kids do something embarrassing it is no longer just the story that spreads and becomes embellished. The photos and videos are spread around and they are spread quickly. In these cases a picture will say far more than 1000 words. It can destroy your kids' reputations' and make their lives miserable. On the plus side, I've learned that the same teens that thrive off of spreading this information have an insatiable appetite to get to the next story and the next embarrassing moment. Because the core teenage behaviour remains the same as years past, this "story" likely will be talked about only until the next person makes an embarrassing move online. Good for one, but bad for all. And it's there forever.

The lost opportunities

There are countless stories of young athletes losing scholarships because of poor behavior online. Sometimes it is from a simple tweet of 140 characters, on Twitter. In other cases it was that photo shared on Instagram. Most of the time, it is because of some ridiculously bad decision that teens make around the world that could have been avoided with some guidance and pause for thought and consequence; only now it has been captured and held, permanently. Simply stated, this is part of being a teenager and we expect them to make mistakes. But consider this: for some of those teenagers; an athletic scholarship may be their only option, when it comes to attending college. So despite a myriad of athletic achievements and potential endorsements from coaches, teammates or even teachers; those college dreams can be wiped out completely in 140 characters or less. Whether you think this is fair or unfair, the reality is that the stakes in these cases are extremely high. And this is our new reality.

My sister received a scholarship from a top-level women's basketball school. Their investment in her involved a lot of resources, energy, time and money. Fortunately, my sister was recruited before social media really blew up into the popular norm that it is today. It is hard to say, but maybe she wouldn't have had that opportunity if the school learned about mistakes she made. My sister was a great kid, but coming from a small town it is unlikely there wouldn't have been photos posted from a party she threw that grew out of hand due to no fault of her own – other than holding the party in the first place of course! What about that first time she tried drinking? Would photos have been posted? Probably. Could that have eliminated her scholarship? It's quite possible and something everyone needs to consider as the sphere of social media continues to grow.

I can think of two popular football programs that faced big scandals due to kids' behaviours. First, the University of Michigan dismissed a sophomore from the team after a video surfaced of him punching a man outside a bar, leaving the man with a broken jaw in three places. You may also consider the case of a University of Oklahoma freshman. One day after turning 18, he allegedly broke four bones in a 20-year-old woman's face when he punched her after allegedly shouting homophobic slurs at a group she was with. Both of these behaviours are violent and when things like this happen, they deserve consequences irrelevant of how the incident is brought to the proper authorities' attention. For all we know, these are good kids who each made one very bad decision. My point is that these incidents were captured and displayed not only for the law enforcement, but for the entire world to see. Beyond the immediate consequences these kids faced, they also would have endured ongoing judgement as the public nature of going "viral" on the Internet also succumbs the participants to the court of public opinion. The consequences of public opinion can be longer lasting and far further reaching than any of us might be able to comprehend.

Only the coaches and University staff know if they did careful research on these players prior to offering them scholarships. Because the risks are so high, universities are now trying to find that quality kid that will also help their program win and social media is one of the fastest tools they can use to learn about potential recruits. Since behaviour online can bring negative attention not only to the person posting but also to an entire organization, people are paying specific attention to how potential recruits may make random comments on social media to determine a young person's character. While hard to really fathom and as unfair as it may seem, judgements are being made on one's suitability for major positions based on single sentences, words and actions. And don't be fooled – this goes for jobs, entrance to programs and even dates! Whether we like it or not, perception tends to be reality for many. All it takes is for someone to whip out their phone in an inopportune moment, and in the next, its gone viral. That's an extreme example, but something we all see now on a regular basis. Seemingly harmless and thoughtless posts, pic, selfie, Tweet, status updates – whatever it may be - can impact one's reputation just as negatively.

Shaping a way forward

In the past, our indiscretions would stay local. Maybe impacting our lives at school, or work – everybody remembers the story of someone who let loose at the office function, but the photos of it (if they exist) have often long since disappeared. In effect, the 'evidence' is gone. We established in the previous chapters that our mistakes could have an impact on us globally and forever. For our kids, that can hurt when applying for college or a job. I am by no means the only one to access Internet for a search of people when they are coming in for an interview. I can find negative things that might give me a reason not to hire an individual, if they exist online. On the other hand, I can focus my search on creative projects, awards, and documentation of service experiences and other things that can be an inspiration to others and can go a long way in setting people apart from others.

Kids can control their online reputations by intentionally carving out positive images of themselves. They can create a blog that highlights the great things they do. They can work to instill the discipline not to post negative things at times when they are angry. They can choose not to post photos in the moment but to wait until they have the chance to think about how it might impact themselves or others. Just as it is human nature for teens to make poor decisions sometimes, in my experience, it is possible to teach them to control those behaviours and begin to redirect them to more positive choices.

ACTIVITY #3

1. Role Model: Many kids are "friends" online with their parents, and it's just as important to be a good role model online as it is in real life. Over-sharing can be risky; think before you post photos and information about your life, and especially about theirs. Take a few minutes to really look at what and how you post. If your kids posted pictures or comments such as you did – would you be proud?

2. Manage Their Digital Footprint: This is ongoing, but you need to regularly check search engines for your child's name and online IDs to see what's appearing there. Remove negative remarks, photos etc., as soon as discovered. Consider setting up a *Google Alert* for regular updates of their web mentions, news etc. Continue maintaining their digital footprint until they are old enough to maintain it for themselves.

3. Make Passwords Private: For most adults, "knowledge is power," but for today's youth, "shared knowledge is power". It is okay for kids to share some things, but they need guidance on how to do it safely. I estimate that nearly 50% of kids in my schools have shared their locker combinations and network passwords with others. Teens commonly do this as a symbol of trust, but if they are sharing these passwords, odds are they are sharing others. Chat with your kids and find out what they already know about identity theft and how to avoid it.

4. Another ongoing activity: You need to remind your kids, "There is no delete button on the Internet". Think of the old cliché, *what happens in Vegas, stays in Vegas* – well, what happens online, stays online.

5. Finally, consider taking control and begin creating a positive identity for your kids at a young age. As shocking as it may seem, it might be smart to register a domain for your child. This helps them establish a foothold online before someone else does.

Raising teens and tweens in today's digitally connected world is complicated. The first impression we give to the world is frequently online. Everything we post on the Internet, and everything posted about us by others, contributes to our overall reputation. While young people can't be expected to fully understand the enormity of all these consequences (who can for that matter?), it is important for families to talk about how to manage their online reputations and to agree on family guidelines. [6]

6

REPUTATION PART II - KEEPING KIDS SAFE ONLINE

This book has been filled with a lot of examples of the risks of Internet behavior. I have also mentioned the importance of teaching children how to act and remain safe online. It is important to acknowledge that there is a world of positive benefits that come in this age of instant access to information. While acknowledging the benefits of online talk and messaging, we must consider scenarios in which we may feel uncomfortable. Whether we encounter inappropriate behavior using the Internet or discover our children may have been victimized somehow, we need to remember that by focusing our children towards positive behaviours, these can directly reflect many of the great things kids do on a regular basis.

In particular, we need to teach them how their online presence reflects three things: (1) how they want to be perceived (2) who they want to be and (3) their influence on the world. [7] Throughout the previous chapters I have stressed that I don't agree with not allowing our children online. Simply put, this is not only unrealistic but it is unreasonable. There are a great number of benefits that kids can enjoy when they do research, interact or generally play online. The way they act online will directly reflect these three important components of their lives. As parents we need to remember this and we need to guide our kids in making safe, moral decisions.

Having said this, I want to be clear that at the same time; I am not condoning an all out, bury your head in the sand, let them do whatever they want approach either. As parents, we would be wise to find a middle ground between completely denying access with not monitoring their activities and/or behavior, at all. The reality is that overly restrictive regulation can prevent kids learning from positive experiences available online, while a laissez faire approach doesn't help kids to make good choices either, because they aren't aware when the bad choices are being made.

Call it the M & M strategy

Just monitoring behaviour alone is not helpful. While it is great to monitor your son's social media activity, if you don't talk to him when he does something you don't approve of, then what's the point? I'm not talking about an immature post that you aren't proud of – kids will say thoughtless stuff online, just like you and I said similar stuff when we were growing up. Although guidance and discussion in these situations can help to set the foundation and guide our kids toward becoming great digital leaders, it is on the harmful stuff you really need to intervene. I'm talking about the stuff that is not only harmful to others, but the damage that is going to harm his future. It is crucial to mediate actively the behaviour that you believe goes against the values of your family.

Taking an active role in *monitoring & mediating* is essential to getting anywhere when talking to your kids about their online behaviour. Think about a time when you were growing up. Your parents likely didn't care for a friend you had. Maybe it was a boyfriend or a girlfriend? Either way, if they banned you from being with those people it likely made you want to be with them even more. Remember, there's a reason *Romeo and Juliet* has been popular for hundreds of years! I don't recommend you monitor in a covert manner. Let your kids know that you are monitoring their activity. Let them know that it is about building trust. Most importantly, let them know you only plan on mediating if they step out of line with those family values. They are the same values expected from face to face interactions and warrant no less guidance, but perhaps more, given the immediateness of the consequences and longstanding effects.

Just like you try to teach your kids how to treat others at a young age, it is important that you communicate with them from the same early age that these expectations extend into the digital world. It won't be an easy conversation if you pull your 16 year-old aside to talk to him or her about their behaviour. If they have spent their formative years being mean or rude to others online, it will be very difficult to get them to change.

The bottom line here is that reputations can be at stake where social media is concerned. But this is a huge opportunity as well. Think about the advantages of portraying ourselves online positively, when as we had said earlier, 'perception is reality'. We can choose to help our children become digital leaders by discussing and guiding them in their online lives, as we do in their day to day interactions. We need to actively bring up and discuss what's going on with them in social media, always tying back to the everlasting footprints we leave behind. Again, this is an opportunity!

The Good News

The good news is that the fact that you are reading this book means you want to develop a plan. Regardless of the age of your kids you need to start to talk to them about your expectations for online behaviour. One can't make the assumption that if they are good with kids face-to-face, they will likewise be good online. Over my years working with kids I have learned a valuable lesson – good kids make bad decisions everyday. I can assure you that my office is not just occupied by "the bad kids". And certainly, it also doesn't mean that the same good kids keep making bad decisions. What it does mean is that kids need guidance and you can help by actively becoming involved in the discussions around appropriateness and values, no matter your confidence level with technology.

The second piece of good news is that aside from learning about *how* to keep you kids safe online, you <u>can</u> learn about the technology they are using. Don't convince yourself that you "can't teach an old dog new tricks". You can figure out what Apps they are using and learn how to navigate the different social media sites on which they are share. I can't stress enough, how important it is to do so.

You might be thinking, how is that good news? I need to sort out this lingo and learn all these sites - I can't afford the time for that! Then I ask you this - can you afford not to? Remember those two athletes who lost their scholarships? How about the two friends who ended up brawling on the high school floor, probably with pictures and videos from multiple sources as an everlasting keepsake? A little bit of your time, some open conversation and you can help your children to not become the next stories.

This set of activities is not meant to be easy. These activities require time to sit down and talk with your kids. Some parents may not feel ready for this and some will find their kids aren't ready. My wife shares a great quote and she reminds me of it on a regular basis – especially in those times when I am avoiding difficult conversations. I will share it with you now because my guess is that many of you may be feeling apprehensive.

"You cannot change the things you refuse to acknowledge."

If you don't like reading that sentence, then I urge you to read it again! Trust me, I hate it when my wife says it to me and that usually means that it is very accurate and I had better take a deep breath and tackle whatever it is that I'm avoiding.

ACTIVITY #4

Moderation

1. Sit down with your kids and look at their postings together. We have recommended you do this in various ways. This time, tell them you will view it as if you're their future employer or college admissions agent, not as a parent.

Mediation

2. Ask *them* to look at their posts as the employer or college admissions agent. If there is foul language, have them read it out loud to you. (I do this with students in parent meetings and it can get pretty uncomfortable when someone has to read something nasty in the presence of mom or dad!)

3. Ask them to copy any posts or images they think are inappropriate onto a blank document. Reposting images with foul language makes them look rude; posting screenshots of gossipy text exchanges makes them seem shallow and mean; posting anything even remotely sexual makes them appear desperate for attention.

4. Copy and paste any of their posts or photos that make you proud. Posting photographs or art can be a great way for kids to express themselves; posting interesting articles or videos can show their intelligence and their interests; heartfelt exchanges with others can show kindness and skill at building community. All of these are VERY important when reinforcing how you want them to act and interact online.

5. Compare the two sets of posts. Have a conversation about whether the negative posts or positive posts form a longer list.
6. Plan a check up in a set period of time. Develop a common goal to move more and more to the pages with the positive reinforcements while eliminating the page with the negatives.

7

SELF IMAGE

The next topic to tackle as it relates to helping our kids thrive as digital citizens pertains to balance and the ill effects of social media. Just as many parents worry about their kids' online behavior, there is the impact that overuse can have with kids who are constantly connected. I'm not going to bore you with data or research: data continues to emerge and be supportive of the impact social media can have on self esteem.

My own observations support that there is a connection to an increase in anxiety and the constant demands placed on kids. For many, their identity is tied to their online persona. How many likes did my Instagram get? Did anyone comment on Facebook post? Was my Tweet retweeted? People will think I'm ignoring them if I don't reply to their SnapChats. In fact, from what I've observed in my daily work and as a parent of a teen, Social Media and constant text messaging have become integral to teenage life for the majority. But I also see a relationship with higher levels of anxiety and lowering of self-esteem among the young people who use them the most.

How can we promote use of these arenas if we believe they contribute to anxiety and lowered self-esteem? I believe that many of these negatives stem, in part, from the fact that we haven't given kids the tools they need to use them wisely. With guidance, tools, and positive learning experiences we can help to guide our kids and not rely solely on Social Media to develop image and identity.

Teens are masters at keeping themselves occupied when they are not engaged in meaningful activity and are idle. Typically they will get online, which can be worse at night when parents are sleeping. During the day, when they're not doing other things (and sometimes even when they are) they're online, on their phones, texting, sharing, trolling, scrolling - you name it. The draw to social media can be constant, which ties us back to the issue of balance, appropriateness, and setting limits.

I remember watching my daughter check her texts while sitting on the bench at her volleyball game. Not a part of our family values and definitely not a positive move in the coach's eyes, as she was promptly benched for the rest of the match. She simply thought that she could steal a glance at her phone and she didn't grasp the fact that even though she was on the bench, it was not the right time to look. After conversations from both the coach and her parents, I am confident she wouldn't make that move again, but at the time I was very bothered by her actions. I began to really think about what was so important, and why I was so bothered by this. After this incident I paid particular attention to the mobile device use by teens in the halls and classes of my school.

One of the realities I came to recognize is that this is simply how kids communicate these days. I think many of us see this and know it to be true, but the pervasiveness can be surprising. Likely my daughter simply wanted to check in to ensure friends didn't think she was ignoring their messages and to see what had transpired in her social world – to stay close to her friends. I realized that I have been guilty about checking texts, email, at inopportune times as well. Times when she would have observed me doing so and assumed that it was ok and the norm. What was lacking in our own home was my own awareness of social media frequency, and conversations about when it is ok, and not ok to quickly check in, in our constantly connected world. I assumed she would know it was not ok to check in mid-game, yet I was modeling similar behaviours. Social media is now a constant and the anxiety it can create can be correlated with the amount and type of use. How this ties to issues with self esteem is that the more we communicate indirectly, the more we're creating opportunities for kids to be anxious.

Self Esteem

Let's reframe image and think about ourselves in photos. Many of us aren't happy with a lot of the pictures taken of us. As adults, the ones we choose to share are the few we have filtered out of the hundreds taken. Now put yourself in your kids' shoes. Pictures are snapped of them all the time. Some are selfies, or group shots and others are just candid pictures that they may have no idea are being taken. Now take away their ability to filter that pic and it becomes posted online for countless others to view. No wonder they feel anxious!

Things haven't changed. Peer acceptance is still one of the biggest concerns for most adolescents. Right or wrong, it is understandable. Their images can end up being posted online, and their image constantly being tied to social media. This is why it is even more important than ever to foster in our children a sense of values, appropriateness and guiding principles online. To treat others online, as they would like to be treated in person.

Teens have always been doing this, but with the advent of social media they are faced with more opportunities—and more traps—than ever before. When kids scroll through their feeds and see how great everyone seems, it only adds to the pressure. Being genuine online can be difficult in the face of so much pressure, but guidance here can help them to project the positive individuals they really are, as opposed to the people they are trying to make people think they are. The more identities they have and the more time they spend pretending to be someone they aren't, the harder it's going to be to feel good about themselves and the cycle of low self esteem can continue.

What should parents do?

I see this as a basic issue. A difficult one for some, or many, of us, but at the heart of much of what I see today. One of the best thing parents can do to minimize the risks associated with technology is to curtail their own consumption first. It's up to parents to set a good example of what healthy computer usage looks like. Most adults check phones or email too much – I can be one of the worst offenders, if left unchecked. Kids should be used to seeing our faces, and not our heads bent over a screen. This may sound like basic parenting, and maybe some of it is, but you would be surprised at how many parents I see in meeting whom are tied to their devices and are not fully paying attention. Think about the message this sends. It is well established that our kids learn from us, and therefore we should lead by example. Again, I see this as a pretty basic, albeit difficult, issue.

Establish technology-free zones or times which parents need to follow as well. Not only does limiting the amount of time you spend plugged in to computers provide a healthy counterpoint to the tech-obsessed world, it also strengthens the parent-child bond and makes kids feel more secure. Kids need to know that you are there for them.

My other recommendation goes back to points laid out earlier. Try to be more involved and discuss the types of social media posts your kids encounter and are involved in, and a discussion about consequences. Not consequences as implied by a negative outcome; certainly negative outcomes abound here. But rather, help to guide your kids regularly about more positively reframing their posts to enhance who they really are. These types of discussions as the 'norm' help to lay the foundation for positive online and social media decisions.

If we are trying to re-shape behaviour and/or instill some of those traditional beliefs around communication, then we need to model the behaviour we want – or maybe more simply put, we need to avoid portraying the behaviour we don't want. This must not be a case of "do as I say, not as a I do".

8

FINAL THOUGHTS and TAKE AWAYS

Throughout this book I've continually gone back to the fact that kids' behaviours at their core are no different that they were 20, 30 even 50 years ago. The way in which they connect, communicate and play out these behaviours is what has changed and continues to change. We used to see the differences between generations but now with the rapid rate that technology advances we are now seeing changes within shorter periods. Regardless of how things evolve, we need to focus on *why* they make the choices they are making. The answer lies in the basis of human nature.

We can put rules in place to monitor our kids' behaviour. We need to do what we can to keep up with how they are playing out these actions. But most importantly, we need to focus on the basic elements covered in the previous chapters - Life-Balance, Ethics, Relationships, Privacy, Reputation and Communication.

Balance

From what I have observed, teens spend more time connected through media than anything else they do on a daily basis - other than sleep – and many sleep fewer hours in a night than the hours that they are connected to media! Most adults wouldn't blame them if they step back and recognize just how interesting this digital world has become. Let's not forget the number of entertainment related activities designed specifically to capture and hold all of our attention. Most of what kids do online is positive and goes on without harm. The challenge is when they are spending too much time with technology. There are studies that indicate children in primary school spend as many hours in front of screens as they do in school!

Learning to balance time spent online with other activities is one of the great challenges we face in the digital age. Learning how to use online time wisely is an important skill we must help our children develop while they are young. Young people look to adult role models to learn how to conduct their online lives, so it's important for us to be mindful of our own time with digital media and lead by positive example. Achieving a healthy balance between all of our activities is a lifelong skill that families need to learn and practice together.

Ethical Behaviour

We know that everyday we are all faced with ethical decisions. As adults we are inundated with even more of these online. For our kids, we hope that face-to-face they will make the right decisions; but imagine how tricky these decisions must be for teens when they are faced with them in the digital world! Without having to face others and physically see the impact of their choices, many young teens are lacking the ethical consideration for others when using the web. It is not their fault because up until now, most teens have never been explicitly taught to learn about and extend their empathy in this virtual realm. The disconnect exists and we need to help them close this gap.

Past generations of teens have learned from help provided by adults to develop their ability to behave ethically toward others. When it comes to digital spaces, kids are teaching adults how to use the tools and as adults we have been largely absent from the online world. This leaves kids still desperately in need for ethical guides in the space they spend the most time.

By talking to our kids we can help them to understand that decisions made today may have lasting consequences. It is vitally important that we have regular discussions about the risk of taking, sending and/or viewing obscene content. Don't be fooled, most kids *know* that it is inappropriate to send sexually suggestive messages to others. Yet over a third of kids I have spoken to send these same messages. And let me tell you; in my role, I can't erase the texts I have read and none of those could be reprinted here!

As we talk to our kids we need them to understand that ethical decisions online can range from sharing an unflattering photo of a friend, to downloading movies and/or music illegally, all the way to sending sexually explicit text and/or images. Kids need to know your family boundaries and what you believe is acceptable use of Internet.

Reputation

If you don't think it is worth the time to talk to your kids, think again. Their reputation (and potentially yours) is at stake with every move they make online.

Remind them that everything posted online including everything that others post about us—contributes to our permanent, digital footprint. This isn't meant to be a scare tactic. It is a fact. And equally important, is the fact that all the good things we are connected to online contribute to a positive reputation!

I really like the notion that kids and adults understand that everything online is persistent, searchable, and replicable. Likewise, it is important to know that largely, we can control all of these things and we can determine if it helps or hurts us when applying for college or a job. Young people likely don't fully understand the enormity of these consequences which is why it is so crucial for us to learn ourselves and then ensure our kids know about managing their online reputations through family guidelines. It could be a great activity to learn together!

Relationships

We all want to help our children grow up having safe and healthy relationships. It can feel disheartening when we face the reality that teens maintain these associations on social media sites, and in online games – not to mention texting! Don't believe me? A former colleague's daughter sent well over 3000 texts messages per month in her final year of high school! We've established that the majority of kids are online in some way. The good news is that in my experience the majority of kids' online relationships is with people they already know. Even more uplifting is the fact that every day I witness kids savour face-to-face interaction. It might look different in that they are carrying on conversations in one another's presence while also connecting with other friends but I would say that social media, is actually creating some things for them to talk about!

Most kids I talk to about poor online behaviour have known that their posts were inappropriate, however they have felt that it was okay because someone else had posted equally inappropriate content. Unfortunately, they usually reference an older sibling and more often than you would think, they reference a parent!

Actually, this is good news for parents. If we can effectively monitor our kids' choices online, modeling appropriate choices is essential just like it is when it comes to your language choices. If you swear at others while you drive, there is a good chance your kids will develop impatience in the car as well. Keep this comparison in mind when you are posting online, if you have considered my advice and you are connected to your kids online, they too can see what you do!

Communication

One of the great concerns that adults have today is the fear that our youth no longer know how to communicate. I have read a number of articles and blog posts indicating worry that they are even destroying the English language. Another colleague I worked with taught me to always look for the positives, therefore; I prefer to view the changing of what is acceptable as the evolution of language versus its destruction. This should all be kept in perspective. At some point in time the French expressions *a la carte* and *a la mode* crept into use amongst English speakers. These expressions are commonplace now, but were likely considered with the same concerns that are expressed about many of the words that are being added to the Oxford Dictionary on an annual basis now. Just because our generation and those before us may not be comfortable with the way in which spelling and grammar are changing, does not mean it is being destroyed. The evolution of language is unavoidable.

The greater issue to focus on regarding communication is the rapid speed with which kids can and expect to communicate. They can reply to others so quickly that the ethics discussed earlier can fly out the window in the blink of an eye. Think about an email you may have sent or received. There is a good chance you can think of something you regret sending. I know I do. The beauty of technology is that we can stop and take a moment to read what we've written. If we can accept that sometimes we are impulsive, then we can also strive to regulate ourselves. Sitting on a reply overnight is a great practice anytime we are feeling angry or upset. If we can teach our kids to follow this pattern it will cut out a whole lot of the drama and anguish caused by impulsive, nasty and inappropriate postings.

The bottom line is that kids today communicate differently than previous generations. It is important for us to talk with them about our values and explain why we have them. It is equally important to respect that while they may uphold these values, it may look drastically different than what you think it should and that is okay.

Technology allows us to communicate more efficiently and (debatably) more effectively than ever before. To conclude, let's embrace this evolution and with our kids, help shape how we move forward positively together.

FINAL THOUGHTS

There are things to be aware of when our kids are online, but at the same time there is plenty of good that can come from time spent there. Kids don't benefit from denial of access and they need to develop the skills to become leaders in a digital world. The rate of evolution of technology is not going to slow anytime soon. With portable devices on everyone's wish list, access to the digital sphere is only going to grow.

With this growth in mind I want to take you back to 3 questions brought up in the Introduction to this book. Whether you did all of the activities or none, whether you talked through some of the scenarios with your kids or you don't feel ready; there are 3 ongoing questions you need to ask your children and these 3 questions can guide your future conversations:

1) How do they want to be perceived? The reputation is still the most important thing to teens. Pause before they post and think about how that post could potentially impact them in the future. More frequently, our digital footprint is our new first impression and it starts taking shape the minute we go online. These are new conversations we need to be having with our kids – let's have them!

2) Who do they want to be? The beauty of this online world is that we can take time to craft the person we wish to be. Take a moment to map out which version of themselves they want others to see. Strategically join a positive hashtag – by this I mean choose a hashtag that your child feels sends their best message such as #beyourbest to highlight the good things they're doing. Another way to create a good impression and positive image is to purposefully post positive pictures on Instagram. Social media is a tool that can be used to practice our happiness habits. Help your child to make it a part of their natural thinking to pause prior to uploading and ask themselves; what do they want to portray in that particular digital image and what the consequences (good and bad) could be.

* Remember - as parents when we do these things, we are modeling for our children.

3) How do they want to influence the world? When kids use social media they can do it for good or for harm. It is that simple. My daughter has tried very hard to remain supportive by positively defending friends if others have posted negatively about them. This does not have to be confrontational; it usually involves something along the lines of "you don't know my friend, she is beautiful and kind..."

There is a real difference between not liking something and having the ability to write or post *why* you aren't supportive. As parents we need to give our kids guidelines and then participate *with* them online. When kids ask us questions about the online world and we don't know the answers, they wonder *why don't you know the answer?* Showing a willingness to find the answer together lets them know you are interested and you will help them by defining boundaries when necessary. When we work with kids they feel most valued when they are part of the conversation. My work has taught me many things, the most important being that kids will almost always reach for the highest expectations we place on them. So, expect the best and then be ready to talk through those times when they don't quite get there. But let's do what we can to help them put their best foot forward online, as a part of their digital identity.

ABOUT THE AUTHOR

John Tyler is an educator with over 20 years of experience working with children and youth of all ages. He gives presentations and speaks to parents and educators on a variety of topics. In 2013 he was recognized as an Apple Distinguished Educator for his leadership in schools. He has two daughters and lives in Vancouver, British Columbia with his wife and their daughter.

ACKNOWLEDGEMENTS

Getting a book to the print/publication stage can be difficult. This process took significantly longer than I had hoped. Competing distractions are numerous. New projects and opportunities are exciting and thus, are easy to say 'yes' to. For those who have learned the art of 'no' while remaining a person open to offers, I applaud you.

Thank you to my loving, patient, incredibly smart, and beautiful wife Angela. Without her encouragement, this would still be at the idea stage.

Also, thank you to my daughters for helping to create the inspiration to write this. My oldest; due to timing, we learned about Social Media alongside one another. My little; This will become innate and a part of your world much earlier. I want to help create a better, safer space for you to play as you learn about the world through online interactions.

Thank you Gordon Li for the chats where we brainstorm about exciting ways to bring new ideas to fruition because it is the right thing to do! Jennifer Mowat-Wahlberg for her care, patience and feedback in the earlier stages of this project. Joe Campbell, Peter Ewens, Brad Ovenell-Carter, and David Overgaard for being critical friends and helping me fine-tune. Jesse Miller for the feedback, conversations, and the time to add your expertise in the form of the forward.

Thank you to the Admin teams I have worked with and all of the great educators who take time to help kids work through the challenges they get themselves into while navigating technology and Social Media. And to the kids – whether I have already worked with you or I will be in the future.

Whenever, producing a list like this, my biggest regret is not including people who were instrumental in completing a task. If you helped me and I have not mentioned you by name, please know that I appreciated your help.

Thank you,
JT

REFERENCES

[1] Haesler, Dan. *Driving Down Social Media Way.*

[2] Nielsen (2011). State of the Media: The Cross-Platform Report Q1 2011: Nielsen.)

[3] http://ikeepsafe.org/be-a-pro/relationships/ *Relationships.* Accessed February 17, 2015.

[4] http://ikeepsafe.org/be-a-pro/reputation/ *Reputation.* Accessed February 28, 2015.

[5] Scheff, Sue. *Smile, Snap, Click and Post (or not): Graduation and Prom Party Digital Dram Footprints.* http://www.huffingtonpost.com/sue-scheff/smile-snap-click-and-post_b_3067990.html Accessed December 11, 2014.

[6] *Reputation Hub.* http://www.cyberwise.org/#!reputation-/cak7 Accessed January 21, 2015.

[7] *Three Ways to Find Happiness on Facebook.* http://greatergood.berkeley.edu/raising_happiness/post/safe_online2 Accessed January 23, 2015

57323222R00048

Made in the USA
Charleston, SC
12 June 2016